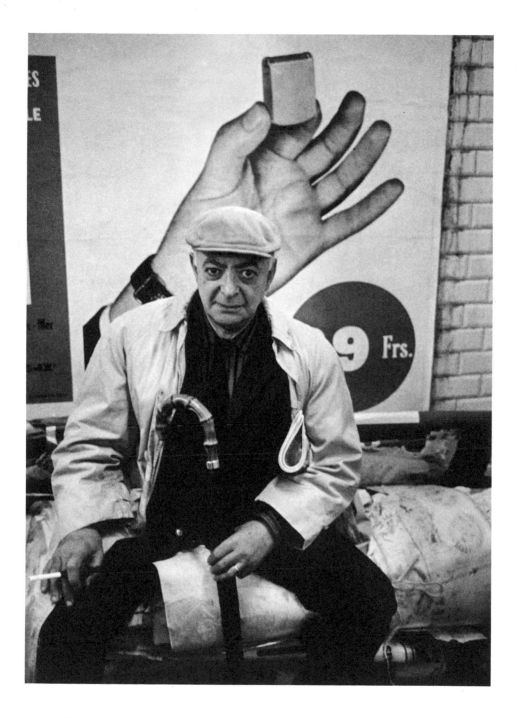

ANDRÉ KERTÉSZ: BRASSAI, 1963

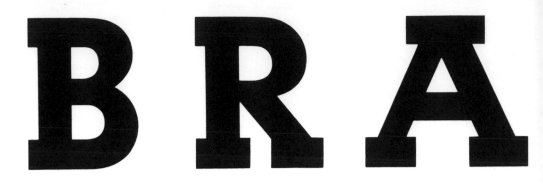

With an introductory essay by Lawrence Durrell

The Museum of Modern Art, New York

Distributed by New York Graphic Society Ltd., Greenwich, Connecticut

Published by The Museum of Modern Art, 1968
11 West 53 Street, New York, New York 10019
All rights reserved
Library of Congress Catalogue Card Number 68-54161
Designed by J. Bourke Del Valle
Printed in Switzerland

THE PHOTOGRAPHY of continental Europe during the past thirty-five years has been polarized by the work of two dominant figures; one is Henri Cartier-Bresson, the other Brassaï. Between them they seem almost to have pre-empted the possibilities of the art in their time and place. Cartier-Bresson has been the classicist, imbued with the French love of measure, valuing balance and clarity and the sophistication of the great tradition—as though he too had decided to do Poussin over again, this time with photography.

Brassaï, the Parisian from Transylvania, seems in contrast an angel of darkness. His sensibility dates from an earlier age, and delights in the primal, the fantastic, the ambiguous, even the bizarre. Yet the most distinguishing characteristic of Brassaï's work is its profound poise and naturalness, its sense of easy permanence. Looking at his pictures, one is not aware of the act of photographing; it is rather as though the subject, through some agency of its own, reproduced itself. This unchallengeable authority is the measure of Brassaï's genius—of his ability to recognize primordial form, and to present his vision with a simplicity that depends on a brilliant and wholly functional technique.

Brassaï was first exhibited at The Museum of Modern Art in 1937, in Beaumont Newhall's pioneering survey *Photography 1839–1937*. Since then, his work has been seen in many Museum exhibitions, most extensively in 1956 in a one-man exhibition of his *Graffiti*.

For their contributions to the current exhibition, and to this book, the Museum gratefully acknowledges its debt, first, to Brassaï himself, for graciously making his own collection available for study and loan; to Charles Rado and Frank Dobo, for assistance with research and bibliographical problems; to André Kertész, for permission to reproduce his portrait of Brassaï (frontispiece); and to Josephine Bush, for editorial assistance. Finally, the Museum's special gratitude is due David H. McAlpin, whose generosity made it possible to acquire for the Museum collection a substantial portion of the work here reproduced.

John Szarkowski
Director, Department of Photography

He is far from being an enigmatic figure in his life, this man who "owns more than two eyes" (to quote Jean Paulhan), who is the "eye of Paris" itself (Henry Miller). There is no great mystery behind the famous pseudonym, unless it be the incidental mystery which surrounds the act of creation: the mystery of its genesis. In the case of Brassaï the photographer, one senses two strong lines of force thrown out by his work—two strong flavors which complement each other. Firstly, that of his sharply selective yet tender treatment of light and dark; secondly, the flavor of the capital city which he adopted as a muse—Paris. He is very much a child of Paris, and in some way the city's most faithful biographer.

In 1923 (he was still called Gyula Halász then) he arrived in Paris as a young painter, fresh from his studies in the art academies of Budapest and Berlin. He was just twenty-four years of age, and like so many other young artists could have described himself as gifted, handsome, and—poor. But poverty is not the end of the world when one is twenty-four; like everyone else he set about making a career for himself. Paris then was very much more of a village than it is today, which perhaps explains the smooth inevitability of Brassaï's conquest of it; he fell among the poets and painters of Montmartre and Montparnasse—young men with names like Picasso and Dali and Braque. The warmth of his personality soon attached them to him and he made friendships then which have lasted until today without a shadow of misunderstanding or rupture. But more important still, from our point of view, was the fact that the possibilities of the camera as a creative instrument were only then being thoroughly explored; Man Ray of course had forged a link with painting by his work, while many another painter was experimenting with film, both still and moving. Picabia, Dali, Cocteau, Buñuel, René Clair.... He had arrived at a time when all kinds of experiments were afoot.

While he wrote and painted he found himself becoming interested in the camera; luckily for us he turned it upon the personalities around him. Today there is hardly a poet or painter of that epoch whose mental image for us has not been touched by some characteristic Brassaï portrait of him when young. It was not only Paris, then, which fired the imagination of this Transylvanian student but also (and almost by accident) the denizens of the capital as well. It was now that he selected his pseudonym, deeming his own name too difficult to spell. He signed his essays and articles with the new name he had coined from that of his native village Brasso in Transylvania. Thus was "Brassaï" born.

Although much has been written about his work, and written with discernment and penetration, he is still the best guide to it, for he is highly articulate and has subjected it to many small autocriticisms which throw into relief his creative attitudes and preoccupations. Yet I would like to describe at first hand a recent Brassaï session because it seems to me to illustrate the ideas of this *maître* even better than his own sharply focused aphorisms.

I was lucky enough last year to receive word from him asking if he might photograph me for an American periodical. I had not seen him since about 1937—and that meeting was a fleeting one; at the time we printed one of his pictures in *The Booster*. But while I did not know him very well he was a close friend of Henry Miller, and indeed figures in *Tropic of Cancer,* as the photographer who showed Miller round Paris by night. Naturally I was delighted and honored to resume this old acquaintance with him; but owing to a muddle over dates Brassaï arrived to find two young American press photographers standing over me, subjecting me to a fusillade of photography. They were both bright boys and industrious, but their idea seemed to be to shoot a million pictures before selecting one for printing. Moreover their equipment was fantastic, elaborate, enormously expensive; I remember a telephoto lens the length of a submarine periscope. Well, into this small cramped cottage wandered Brassaï with his air of attentive vagueness. He had hardly any equipment at all, one very old camera with a cracked lens hood, a tripod which kept kneeling down like a camel—really amazing equipment, but as cherished as it was venerable.

"After twenty years you can begin to be sure of what a camera will do." Undeterred by honest competition, he sat and had a *pastis* while the young men prowled about, snapping and clicking, fussing about with the lights and swearing amiably. I do not know how they discovered who he was—perhaps his name came up by accident. But the change that came over them was quite extraordinary, for they were fans of his. Was it really him, they asked, feeling him all over? Then they shamefacedly hid all their equipment in the garage and made room for Brassaï's venerable antique. They were men of tact and modesty. They asked humbly if they might watch him in action. Brassaï of course was delighted; he maundered about scattering cigar ash from his white bone holder. After several attempts worthy of Laurel and Hardy we managed to get the tripod to stand up. Brassaï found the light too harsh; we turned almost everything off. The camera, it appeared, was fond of shadow. Well, with this vexing business of light regulated, and his camera aimed at me in a corner of the sofa, Brassaï sighed and sat down in his chair, for all the world as if he had finished the job and was relaxing for a smoke. But he had not begun. Quietly, absently he started to talk to the Americans about photography in general, all the time keeping track of me with that hawk's eye. While he talked he reflected. If I remember much of what he said it is because I had to translate it for him, as he speaks no English. The tenor of his discourse was roughly as follows: "Yes, I only take one or two or three pictures of a subject, unless I get carried away; I find it concentrates one more to shoot less. Of course it's chancy; when you shoot a lot you stand a better chance, but then you are subjecting yourself to the law of accident—if accident has a law. I prefer to try and if necessary fail. When I succeed, however, I am much happier than I would be if I shot a million pictures on the off-chance. I feel that I have really made it myself, that picture, not won it in a lottery." All the time he was watching me, studying me in a vague and absent-minded fashion. He went on, with a motion to me to tell me to continue my running translation. "Another thing today is to try and trap your subject off his guard, in the erroneous belief that you will reveal something special about him if you do so. This leads to tricks in the end. I don't do things that way. I can't."

He made some minor alteration of stance to his tripod, still smoking and talking in his soft mellifluous voice—as if talking to himself. "On the contrary I want my subject to be as fully conscious as possible—fully aware that he is taking part in an artistic event, an *act*. Do you remember the old cameras that the village photographer used at the turn of the century? Large as an oak tree, with a lens cap the size of a cat's face, and a billowing black hood? All the village came to have marriage and confirmation pictures taken. It was a solemn, almost holy event. You were obliged to sit still; with the old lens cap the exposure was sometimes four seconds. Moreover, you had to hold your breath, sit still, and stare 'at the dicky bird.' The fact that it was ritual did something to the sitter—you can see the souls looking out of their faces more easily than you can in our photographs of today. They were not off guard, but fully cooperative, sharing an act of innocent majesty—'having a picture took.' That is what I still try and hunt for." Suddenly, with a surprisingly agile movement across the room the *maître* came up to me and said: "There, just like that; just what I want. Now!" I had apparently moved into a position which suited his book. He sat down, focused, and told me to look dead into the camera and hold it. Only when he approved of the expression on my face did he fire. And that was all for the day.

I suggest that this is very much what he was trying to express when, in the course of an interview for Paris Radio, he said: "I don't bother myself with psychology. I photograph everything—one doesn't need psychology.... When I do a picture of someone I like to render the immobility of the face—of the person thrown back on his own inner solitude. The mobility of the face is always an accident.... But I hunt for what is permanent." One feels the invisible quotation marks round the word "psychology"; Brassaï does not "interpret" but allows the subject to interpret itself on his film. His only task is to open the door, so to speak, on the experience, to choose his moment, and then to press the trigger.

In some notes he has put down about himself I find the following passages which are interesting not only in the way they touch on his intentions, but also for the few technical ideas buried in them. "I came late," he writes, "to photography; until my thirtieth year I knew nothing about it—indeed, I rather despised it. And I never had a camera in my hand. It all came about because I am a noctambulist *(je ménais une vie noctambule)*; and the aspects of the capital at night fired and excited me. How on earth, I asked myself, could I capture and fix these powerful impressions—by what medium? I had been haunted for years by these fugitive images. My friend André Kertész broke the spell by lending me a camera; I followed his advice and his example. So was *Paris by Night* put together. I transformed my hotel room into a laboratory. I bought *(à crédit)* a really good camera—the Bergheil by Voigtlander, 6.5 by 9 cm., with the Heliar f/4.5 lens. For long months I only shot at night. By the way, I have always been faithful to this camera. I have always done my own developing and printing and enlarging. Of all printing papers I love the glossy—it's the only type which tells you straight away that you have to do with a photograph and nothing else. I think you will be able to judge for yourself about my favorite subject-matter; it's self-evident from the work. But I only want to emphasize the extremely practical considerations which provoked me to learn to photograph. On the other hand I would like to add something else: I've always had a horror of specialization in any one medium. That is why I have constantly changed my medium of expression—photo, drawing, cinema, writing, theater decor, sculpture, engraving.... And I've published about fifteen books, no two of which are alike."

He has to satisfy, then, a protean temperament, and he does so to the full; the really remarkable thing is that he succeeds in fulfilling himself in all these media— he is a powerful draftsman, sculptor, and so on. One would imagine that all these secondary modes of expression would be hobbies like Sunday painting for a writer. Not a bit of it. He contends with his peers in every field.

But with an artist as articulate as Brassaï it is a crime not to let him speak for himself as much as possible, and this I propose to do now with some selections from his voluminous writings and commentaries on his own work. It is not merely that the *data* is interesting in itself, it is also the angle of vision. One can see *why* a Picasso and a Braque cherish a fellow artist of this caliber; when he does an interview the questions he puts are a joy to listen to—and to answer. That is why his *Conversations with Picasso* is such an invaluable guide to the painter's ideas about his art.

"For me the photograph must suggest rather than insist or explain; just as a novelist offers his readers only a part of his creation—in leaving certain aspects unexpressed—so I think the photograph shouldn't provide superfluous explanations of its subject. I'm thinking for example of certain façades of old houses, pierced with windows which no human presence could ever bring alive. Without knowing more about it I can imagine the sort of existence human beings lead behind walls like these. But better still, I should be able, by photographing it in a certain way to render completely tangible the hidden life behind."

"The photograph has a double destiny.... It is the daughter of the world of externals, of the living second, and as such will always keep something of the historic or scientific document about it; but it is also the daughter of the rectangle, a child of the *beaux-arts*, which requires one to fill up the space agreeably or harmoniously with black-and-white spots or colors. In this sense the photograph will always have one foot in the camp of the graphic arts, and will never be able to escape the fact. Indeed in every photo you will find the accent placed either on the side of document or of the graphic arts. It's inescapable. At the beginning, of course, photography began to imitate the various schools of painting but at the time when I started work it had already begun to shake off the shackles of the purely pictorial. In each country we saw a reaction set in with the work of one man—Stieglitz in the U.S.A., Emerson in England, Atget in France.... With them the document yielded up its place, likewise the preoccupation with painting; photography became purely itself, neither less nor more. That is to say that people began to produce images in this medium which could not be produced in any other way whatsoever. As for those who asked (and still ask) in what the photograph differs from every other medium I reply by referring them to the scrap of conversation with Picasso which I have quoted in my book."

In the conversation referred to Picasso said: "When one sees what you manage to express by a picture one suddenly realizes just how much is no longer a concern of painting.... Why should an artist obstinately keep on trying to render something which can be rendered so well by the lens? It would be silly, no? Photography has come to its present state in order to free painting from all literature, all anecdote, and even subject matter.... The painters should profit by their recovered liberty to do something else."

In these passages Brassaï is very much the explicit artist, conscious of what he is attempting; but in others he is not above launching an epigram with a double take embedded in it. I am thinking of his declaration: *"Je n'invente rien, j'imagine tout"* (I invent nothing, I imagine everything). Such a *boutade* underlines the need for intuition marching hand in hand with sympathy—not merely the powers of a frigid intelligence. In other words he lays himself open always to the creative accident; his mind may organize, but it is his intuition which pierces the carapace of the material object to reveal its symbolic properties.

Yet when all is said and done Brassaï remains with us, in life; even when he does a still life the object echoes on, vibrates with the warmth of its human association. His little park chair is empty, yes; but the man or woman who sat there all afternoon has suddenly got up and left, so recently that if you put your hand on the tin seat you could feel the fugitive warmth of the body. If Brassaï photographs a branch of plum blossom it is still vibrating from the weight of the bird which has at this very moment elected to disappear. The human association makes him a human biographer, whether he is dealing with Paris, or with a subject like graffiti, or with "those empresses of the night," cats. He is a totally besotted catomane, Brassaï, though mysteriously enough he does not seem to own one of his own. At least I have found no trace of it in the two Paris studios where he works. Perhaps (knowing him) he prefers one of the terrifying temple cats in stone from the museum. I can imagine him standing before it for hours, drinking it in.

Even an abstract subject like graffiti, the subject of his best book (in my opinion) does not render his work objective, withdrawn, cold. Despite the absence of a human subject the pictures vibrate with warmth and coherence. Especially if one has stumbled upon a chance remark of his from the catalogue of a Paris exhibition: *"Le mur m'attire aussi par ses graffiti parce que, dans notre civilisation, il remplace la nature"* (Walls attract me by their graffiti, because, in our civilization, they replace nature). An astonishing way of looking at things! But for the men of the cities, how true!

I cannot bring this short essay to a close without giving the reader Brassaï's own account of his first venture into moving film. It begins like a fairy story: "One day, deciding to try out my capacity as a *cinéaste* I bought a camera and took it along to the zoo." The result of this excursion was a great success, winning a prize at Cannes, and getting itself distributed in about seven countries. But what he has to say about the adventure is, as always, of paramount interest in its relation to his work: "I wanted to track down the fundamental difference between the photograph and the film. Contrary to what one imagined the photograph doesn't express movement; on the contrary, it *arrests* it.... And the more one increases the speed of the shutter the more definitive is the stoppage.... It's here that photography pushes us out of the ordinary range of human perception towards the scientific domain. I've often thought that photography was closer to sculpture than to music, because sculpture also arrests movement.... On the other hand the cinema is movement itself; no picture subsists all by itself, but as a function of the one just before and the one behind. In this sense the greatest enemy of the real cinema is the ability to make marvelous photographs as, say, the Mexicans do. My own little film is all movement, and in order to underline the sovereignty of movement, I cut out all words, all commentary.... A little music to accompany the movement of the animals, that was all. I even went so far as to prevent myself consciously from trying to 'compose' beautiful photographs; I snuffed out the still photographer in myself in remembering that the cinema is *movement*."

This, then, is the creative history of a singular artist of our times, whose work excites and warms us by its humanity and insight. Yet the story is far from ended, for Brassaï has vast plans for the future. In the last few years he has begun to devote a great deal more time to sculpture, and this new aspect of his work has won him new admirers and the promise of a series of exhibitions. As for photography, here also we have been promised further work to come—work of which a mountain still awaits publication among his files. From those laborious years '32, '33, and '34 a very small selection was made to illustrate *Paris by Night*; the great bulk of his work of this period remains unprinted. Now, in a totally changed Paris of 1968, these pictures have taken their place in history and merit a much larger audience than the original book had. Brassaï plans to give them to us soon. It must be a strange feeling to be still alive and yet to feel so sure that one is part of the history of one's epoch. Brassaï, like his friends, can draw comfort from the thought that the effort was worth it, that the game is won.

Lawrence Durrell

GATE OF THE JARDIN DU LUXEMBOURG, 1932

OPPOSITE: GALA SOIRÉE AT MAXIM'S, 1946–1947

ABOVE: GROUP IN A DANCE HALL, 1932

19

ABOVE: AVENUE DE L'OBSERVATOIRE, 1932

OPPOSITE: NUIT DE LONGCHAMPS, 1936

OPPOSITE: ALONG THE SEINE, 1932

ABOVE: MAN SLEEPING, 1932

23

GRAFFITI, n.d.

JEAN GENÊT, 1955

TWO HOODLUMS, 1932

SEVILLE, SPAIN, 1952–1953

VALLAURIS, 1948

BALEARIC ISLANDS, 1953

AMBROISE VOLLARD, 1932

GERMAINE RICHIER, 1958

ABOVE: GRAFFITI, n.d.

OPPOSITE: PICASSO, RUE DE LA BOÉTIE, 1932

MARKET PORTER, LES HALLES, 1939

GIRL PLAYING SNOOKER, MONTMARTRE, 1933

KIKI SINGING IN A MONTPARNASSE CABARET, 1933

STREETWALKER, 1932

BROTHEL, RUE QUINQUEMPOIX, 1933

BONNARD, LE CANNET, 1952

TRAMP IN MARSEILLE, 1937

STREET FAIR, 1933   41

AVENUE DE L'OBSERVATOIRE, 1934

PLACE DE LA CONCORDE, 1945

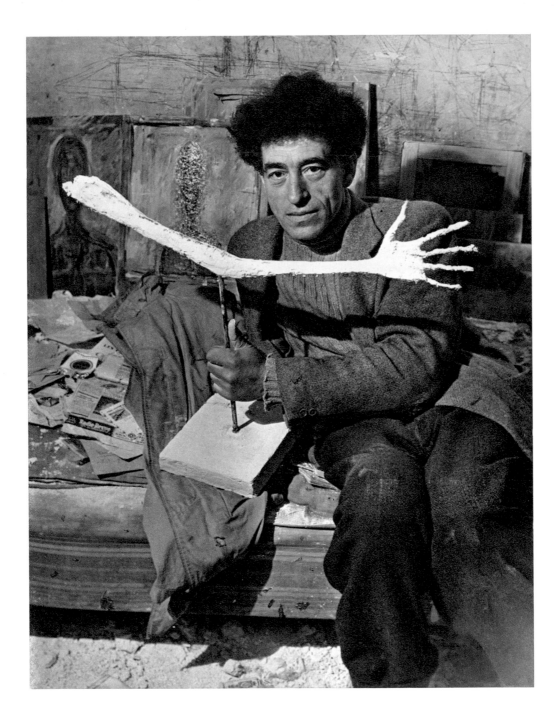

GIACOMETTI, 1934

GRAFFITI, n.d.

ABOVE: FOLIES-BERGÈRE, 1932

OPPOSITE: CHARTRES IN WINTER, 1946

Une Tenue
Correcte
est de Rigueur

ABOVE: BAL TABARIN, 1932

OPPOSITE: PONT DES ARTS, 1934

THE ROYAL SHOW, ENGLAND, 1959

"PÈRE LA FLÛTE" IN THE MÉTRO, 1938

BUTTRESS OF THE ELEVATED, 1938

PONT NEUF, 1949

ABOVE: FEMALE COUPLE, 1932

OPPOSITE: PLANE TREE, PARIS, 1938

GRAFFITI, n.d.

SALVADOR DALI, 1933

PRISON WALL OF LA SANTÉ, 1932

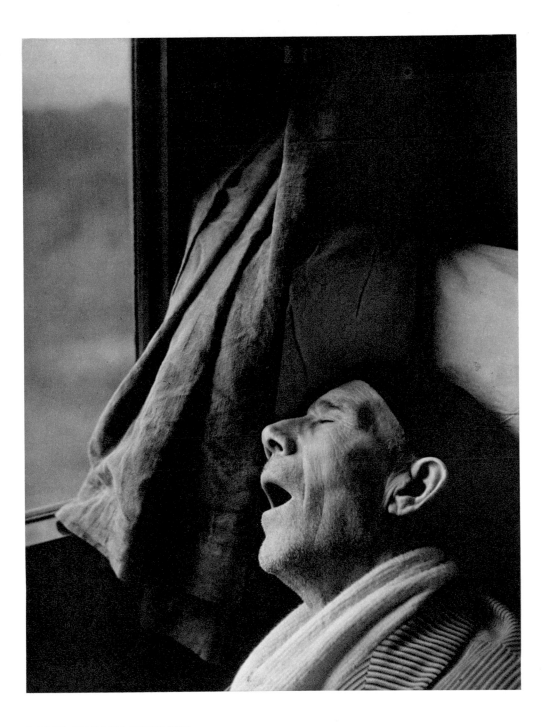

ROME–NAPLES EXPRESS, 1955

PARC MONTSOURIS, 1931

64

CHRISTMAS EVE MASS, LES BAUX, PROVENCE, 1945

ABOVE: RUE QUINQUEMPOIX, 1932

OPPOSITE: QUARREL, 1932

GRAFFITI, n.d.

GRAFFITI, n.d.

GRAFFITI, n.d.

PIMP AND GIRL, 1933

GRAFFITI, n.d.

HENRY MILLER, 1932

GRAFFITI, n.d.

MADAME MARIANNE D.-B., 1936

"BIJOU" OF MONTMARTRE, 1932

SELECTED BIBLIOGRAPHY COMPILED BY BRUCE K. MACDONALD
Note: All illustrations cited are by Brassaï.

BOOKS AND OTHER GENERAL WORKS

1. ADHÉMAR, J. *et al. Brassaï.* Paris: Bibliothèque Nationale, 1963, 27 pp. plus 1 illus. (on cover). Exhibition catalogue.

2. AUBIER, DOMINIQUE. *Séville en fête.* Paris: Robert Delpire, 1954, 152 pp. incl. 140 illus.
German ed.: *Fest in Sevilla* (Feldafing, Obb., West Germany: Buchheim-Verlag, 1954); English ed.: *Fiesta in Seville* (London: Thames and Hudson, 1956).

3. BRASSAÏ. "The Art of the Wall," in John Hadfield, ed., *The Saturday Book, 18.* New York: Macmillan, 1958, pp. 237–240 plus 15 illus.
Translated from the French by James Clark.

4. ————. *Brassaï.* Paris: Éditions Neufs, 1952, [81] pp. incl. 58 photographs, 8 drawings, 8 sculptures.
Introduction by Henry Miller; essay, "Souvenirs de mon enfance," and "Notes" by Brassaï.

5. ————, ed. *Brassaï présente images de camera.* Paris: Hachette, 1964, 255 pp. incl. 1 illus.
Introduction by Brassaï.

6. ————. *Camera in Paris.* London and New York: The Focal Press, 1949, 95 pp. incl. 62 illus.

7. ————. *Conversations avec Picasso.* Paris: Gallimard, 1964, 334 pp. plus 53 illus.
Reviewed in bibl. 60. English ed.: *Picasso and Company* (Garden City, N.Y.: Doubleday & Co., 1966, 289 pp. plus illus.).

8. ————. "Four French Photographers," in *U.S. Camera 1953.* New York: U.S. Camera Publishing Corp., pp. 9–31, 62 incl. 20 illus.
Introduction by Edward Steichen.

9. ————. *Graffiti.* Stuttgart: Chr. Belser Verlag, 1960, 47 pp. plus 105 illus.

10. ————. *L'histoire de Marie.* Paris: Point du Jour, 1949, 85 pp.
Introduction by Henry Miller.

11. ————. "Language of the Wall," in *U.S. Camera 1958.* New York: U.S. Camera Publishing Corp., pp. 6–15, 290, 294 incl. 48 illus.
Statement by Edward Steichen.

12. ————. *Language of the Wall: Parisian Graffiti Photographed by Brassaï.* London: Institute of Contemporary Arts, 1958, 12 pp. incl. 4 illus.
Exhibition catalogue. Introduction by Roland Penrose; essay by Brassaï.

13. ————. *Paris de nuit.* Paris: Arts et Métiers Graphiques, [1933], 12 pp. plus 62 illus.

14. ————. *Tant qu'il y aura des bêtes.* Two-reel film, black-and-white, 16 mm., sound. Paris, 1955.
Print in The Museum of Modern Art, Department of Film. *See* bibl. 28.

15. ————. *Transmutations.* Lacoste (Vaucluse), France: Galerie Les Contards, 1967, portfolio of 12 *clichés-verres.*
Introduction by Brassaï.

16. ————. *Trente dessins, poème de Jacques Prévert.* Paris: P. Tisné, 1946, 11 pp. plus 28 illus.
————. *See also* bibl. 24.

17. KAHNWEILER, DANIEL HENRY. *Les sculptures de Picasso.* Paris: Les Éditions du Chêne, 1948, [13] pp. plus 218 illus.
English ed.: translated by A. D. B. Sylvester (London: Rodney Phillips, 1949).

18. KOCHNO, BORIS. *Soirée de ballets.* Paris: Les Éditions du Chêne, 1945, [16] pp. incl. 8 illus.
Photographs by Brassaï used as stage design.

19. MILLER, HENRY. *Max and the White Phagocytes.* Paris: Obelisk Press, 1938, pp. 240–252.
For first part of this essay, in French, *see* bibl. 59.

20. ————. *Quiet Days in Clichy.* Paris: Olympia Press, 1956, 171 pp. plus 26 illus.
————. *See also* bibl. 4, 10, 42, 59.

21. POLLACK, PETER. *The Picture History of Pho-*

tography. New York: Harry N. Abrams, 1958, pp. 404–417 incl. 10 photographs, 1 drawing, 2 sculptures.

Italian ed.: *Storia della Fotographia* (Milan: A. Garzanti, 1959, pp. 426–439); French ed.: *Histoire mondiale de la photographie* (Paris: Librairie Hachette, 1961, pp. 406–419); German ed.: *Die Welt der Photographie* (Dusseldorf: Econ-Verlag, 1962, pp. 366–375).

22. RUSSELL, JOHN. *Paris.* New York: Viking Press, 1960, 264 pp. incl. 42 illus.

23. SOUCEK, LUDVÍK. *Brassaï.* Prague: Státní Nakladatelství Krásné Literatury a Umění, 1962, [31] pp. plus 61 illus.

24. STETTNER, LOUIS. *10 Photographs by Louis Stettner.* Paris and New York: Two Cities Publications, 1949, (no pagination).

Edition limited to 250 copies. Introduction in French and English by Brassaï (*see* bibl. 31).

25. VINDING, OLE. *Farlig Fred.* Copenhagen: K. E. Hermans Forlag, 1945, pp. 115–118 illus.

ARTICLES AND REVIEWS

26. AUBERT, CLAUDE. "Les poupées lucides," *Labyrinthe* (Geneva), May 15, 1945, pp. 4–5 incl. 7 illus.

27. "Brassaï," *Photography* (London), February 1962, pp. 24–25 incl. 14 illus.

28. BRASSAÏ. "Brassaï Makes a Movie," *Popular Photography* (New York), April 1957, pp. 84–85, 184–185.

Includes 11 frames from *Tant qu'il y aura des bêtes* (*see* bibl. 14).

29. ———. [Photographs], in *Coronet Magazine* (Chicago), September 1937 through December 1942, *passim.*

30. ———. "Graffiti parisiens," *XXᵉ Siècle* (Paris), March 1958, pp. 21–24 incl. 5 illus.

31. ———. "Louis Stettner," *Camera* (Lucerne), December 1949, pp. 377–382.

Text in German, French, and English (*see* bibl. 24).

32. ———. "Du mur des cavernes au mur d'usine," *Minotaure* (Geneva), no. 3–4, 1933, pp. 6–7 incl. 2 illus.

33. ———. "My Friend André Kertész," *Camera* (Lucerne), April 1963, pp. 7–32.

34. ———. "Paris by Night," *Picture Post* (London), January 21, 1939, pp. 20–27 incl. 32 illus.

35. ———. "La photographie n'est pas un art?" *Le Figaro Littéraire* (Paris), October 21, 1950, p. 6. Reply to bibl. 45.

36. ———. "Le procès de Marie," *Labyrinthe* (Geneva), December 1946, pp. 8–9 incl. 1 illus.

37. ———. "Le sommeil … photos," *Labyrinthe* (Geneva), November 15, 1945, p. 11 incl. 8 illus.

38. ———. "La tourterelle et la poupée," *Labyrinthe* (Geneva), May 15, 1945, p. 9 incl. 8 illus.

39. ———. "Walls of Paris," *Harper's Bazaar* (New York), July 1953, pp. 42–45 incl. 6 illus.

40. ———. "La Villa Palagonia, une curiosité du baroque sicilien," *Gazette des Beaux-Arts* (Paris), September 1962, pp. 351–364 incl. 7 illus.

41. ——— and J. HERBAIR. "Technique de la photographie de nuit," *Photo-Ciné-Graphie* (Paris), January 1934, pp. 2–5 incl. 4 illus.

42. ——— and HENRY MILLER. "Paris la nuit," *Evergreen Review* (New York), May–June 1962, pp. 12–22 incl. 8 illus.

43. CABANNE, PIERRE. "Brassaï: J'imagine tout," *Arts* (Paris), May 22–28, 1963, p. 11.

44. CALLES, ANDRÉ. "Brassaï, le magicien a mis pour nous le monde dans des boîtes," *Combat* (Paris), July 18, 1949, p. 2.

45. CHAPELAN, MAURICE. "Baudelaire avait raison, la photographie n'est pas un art," *Le Figaro Littéraire* (Paris), October 14, 1950, p. 1. *See* bibl. 35.

46. DESCARGUES, PIERRE. "Brassaï chez Picasso," *Les Lettres Françaises* (Paris), November 19–25, 1964, p. 13.

47. DE SOLIER, RENÉ. "Cartier-Bresson, Brassaï et autres gens d'images," *La Nouvelle Nouvelle*

Revue Française (Paris), March 1, 1956, pp. 543–545.

48. Eisner, Maria Giovanna. "Brassaï," *Minicam Photography* (Cincinnati), April 1944, pp. 20–27, 74–76 incl. 8 illus.

49. Gindertael, R.V. "La conscience au pied du mur," *XXᵉ Siècle* (Paris), December 1962, pp. 83–86 incl. 5 illus.

50. Grégory, Claude. "Deux hommes et leurs images: Brassaï … Man Ray," *Arts* (Paris), March 7, 1952, p. 10 incl. 1 illus.

51. Grenier, Roger. "Hommes: Avec Brassaï," *Le Nouvel Observateur* (Paris), November 19, 1964, p. 24.

52. Kasser, Hans. "Paris as Seen by the Camera," *Camera* (Lucerne), September 1949, pp. 259–272 incl. 7 illus.
    Text in German, French, and English.

53. Kertész, André. "Brassaï: Portfolio and an Appreciation," *Infinity* (New York), July 1966, pp. 3–13 incl. 9 illus.

54. Lepage, Jacques. "Brassaï ou l'œil insatiable," *Aujourd'hui* (Paris), April 1965, p. 41.

55. Masclet, Daniel. "Brassaï l'homme de la foule," *Le Photographe* (Paris), March 5, 1952, pp. 78–81 incl. 2 illus.

56. Mauriac, François. "Télévision: Brassaï, il chasse l'homme avec amour," *L'Express* (Paris), November 10, 1960, p. 36.

57. Mourgeon, Jacques. "Télévision: Brassaï, poète de la photo," *Combat* (Paris), November 5–6, 1960, p. 3.

58. Newhall, Nancy. "Brassaï: 'I Invent Nothing, I Imagine Everything,'" *Camera* (Lucerne), May 1956, pp. 185–215 incl. 27 illus.
    Text in French and English.

59. Nieting, Valentin (pseudonym for Henry Miller). "L'œil de Paris," *Delta* (Paris), September 1937, pp. 21–25.
    For a continuation of this essay, in English, *see* bibl. 19.

60. Nourissier, François. "Le livre de la semaine: Conversations avec Picasso," *Les Nouvelles Littéraires* (Paris), November 26, 1964, p. 2 incl. 1 illus.
    Review of bibl. 7.

61. Parella, Lew, ed. "Brassaï: Faithful Chronicler of Life," *U.S. Camera* (New York), February 1955, pp. 77–83 incl. 18 illus.

62. Putnam, Jacques. "Graffiti vus par Brassaï," *XXᵉ Siècle* (Paris), February 1962, suppl. (no pagination) incl. 1 illus.

63. Rado, Charles. "2 Paris Photographers," *Modern Photography* (Cincinnati), February 1950, pp. 50–55, 114 incl. 3 illus.

64. Shapiro, Karl. "Brassaï: Poetic Focus on France," *Art News* (New York), February 1955, pp. 46–47 incl. 6 illus.

65. Stettner, Irving. "A Visit to Brassaï," *Photo Notes* (New York), Fall 1948, pp. 9–13 incl. 1 illus.

FRONT COVER: TRAMP IN MARSEILLE, 1937

BACK COVER: STREET FAIR, 1933